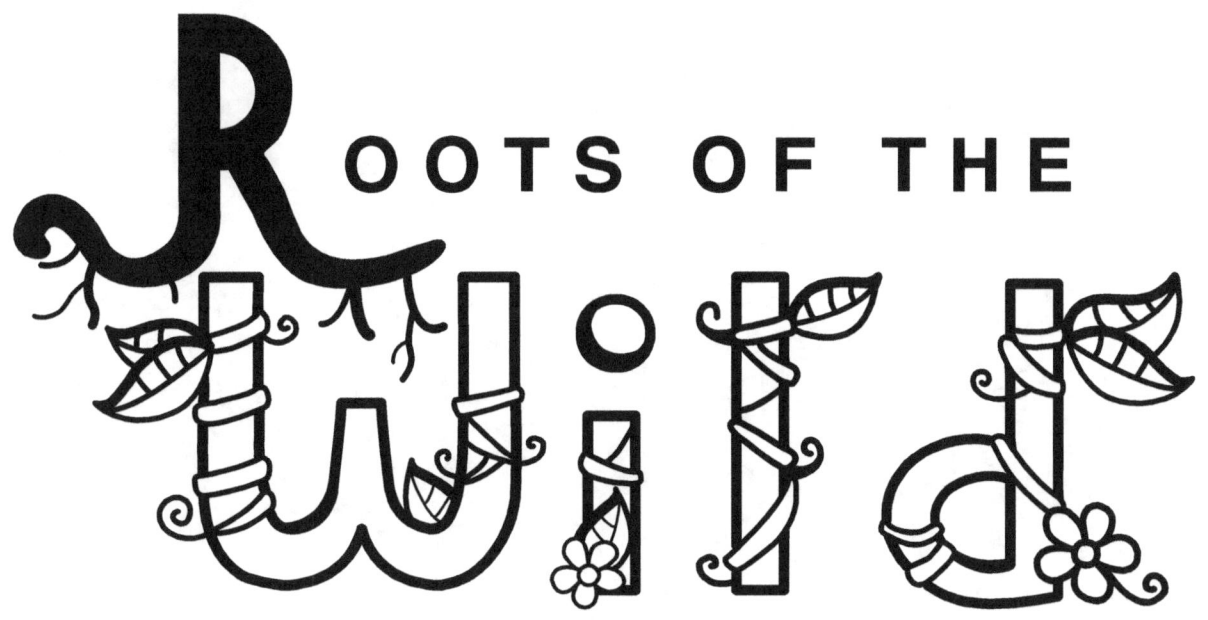

Roots of the Wild

A coloring adventure for all

Jeanette Wummel

Coloring Tip:

When coloring with markers place a piece of paper between pages to prevent bleeding to your next design.

Acknowledgments

So many wonderful and amazing people have supported me through the creation of this book. I would like to specifically thank my family for putting up with all the craziness and for all their love and support.

I would like to thank my husband, Casey Wummel, who encouraged me to continue when I wanted to quit.

I would like to thank my grandparents, who raised me and supported my dreams. Especially to my grandfather, who created my passion for art.

I want to give a special thank you to all those that helped fund my dream to become a reality. Without you this book would not have happened.

Thank you: Pam, Katie Newton, Tracy Cherf/Harley Quinn, Natalie, RoMo, Susanna Rosencrantz, Lisa S., Pam Borek, Kelly Gunaji, Jess Gomersall, DaddyOtis, Autumn Cameron, Meghan Webb-Wagg, Lori Piper, Toni Placensia, Verity Ryan, Lisa Arndt, Daunell Barton, megan, Shannon Jones, TStafford, Adult Coloring Worldwide, Katie and Matt Lloyd, Annie Whittle, Lottie, George, Edward, Max and India, James Soliman, Uncle Chris, Tracy E. Files, Macia Davidson, Amanda McDaniel, Thomas Custer, Lisa, Nichole Pogo, Nadine Mesick, Kza, Vivian Kwan, Kellie Brabec, Jen Irwin, Kelli Murphy, Addison McCleskey, and Mina

Copyright

This book belongs to

_____

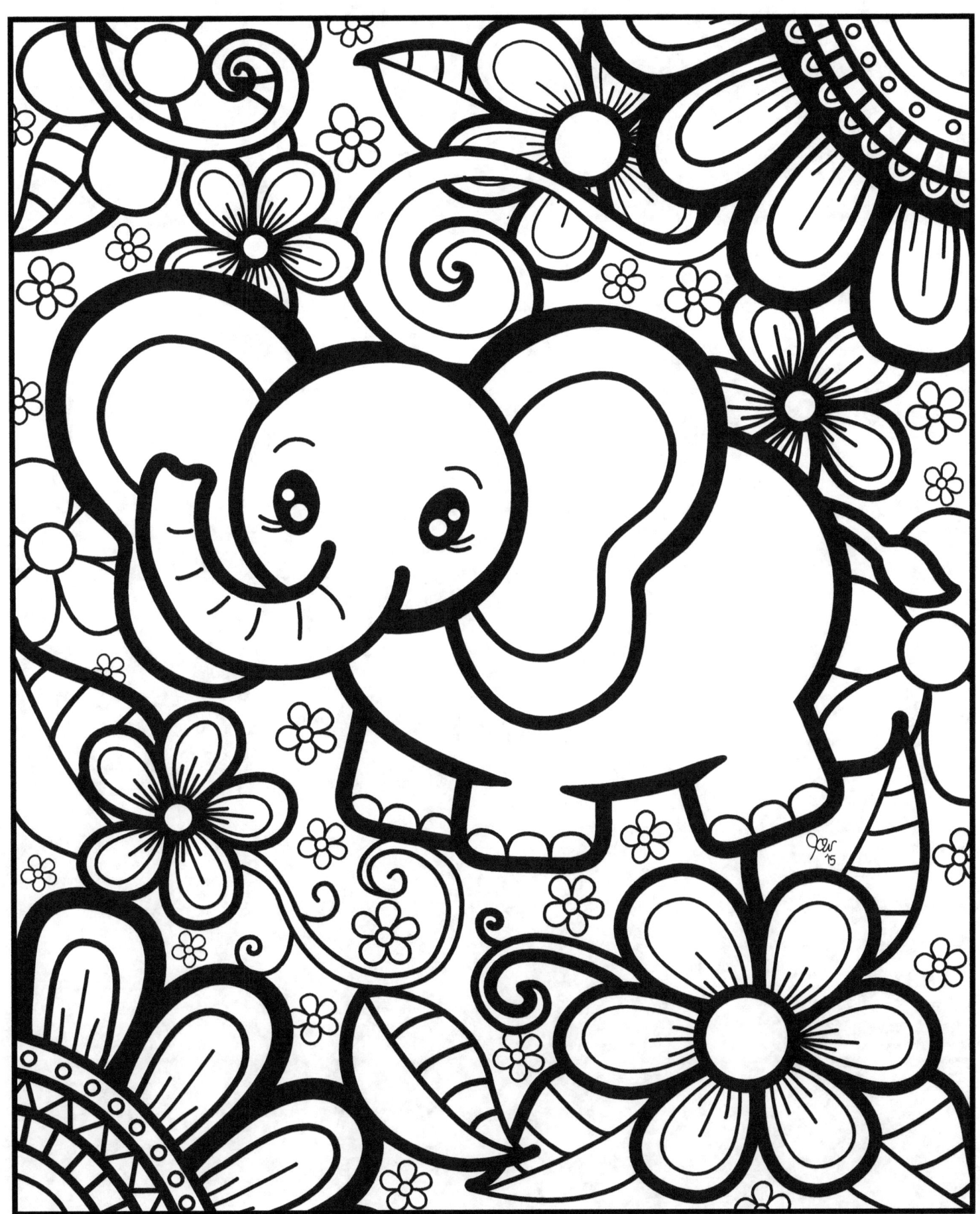

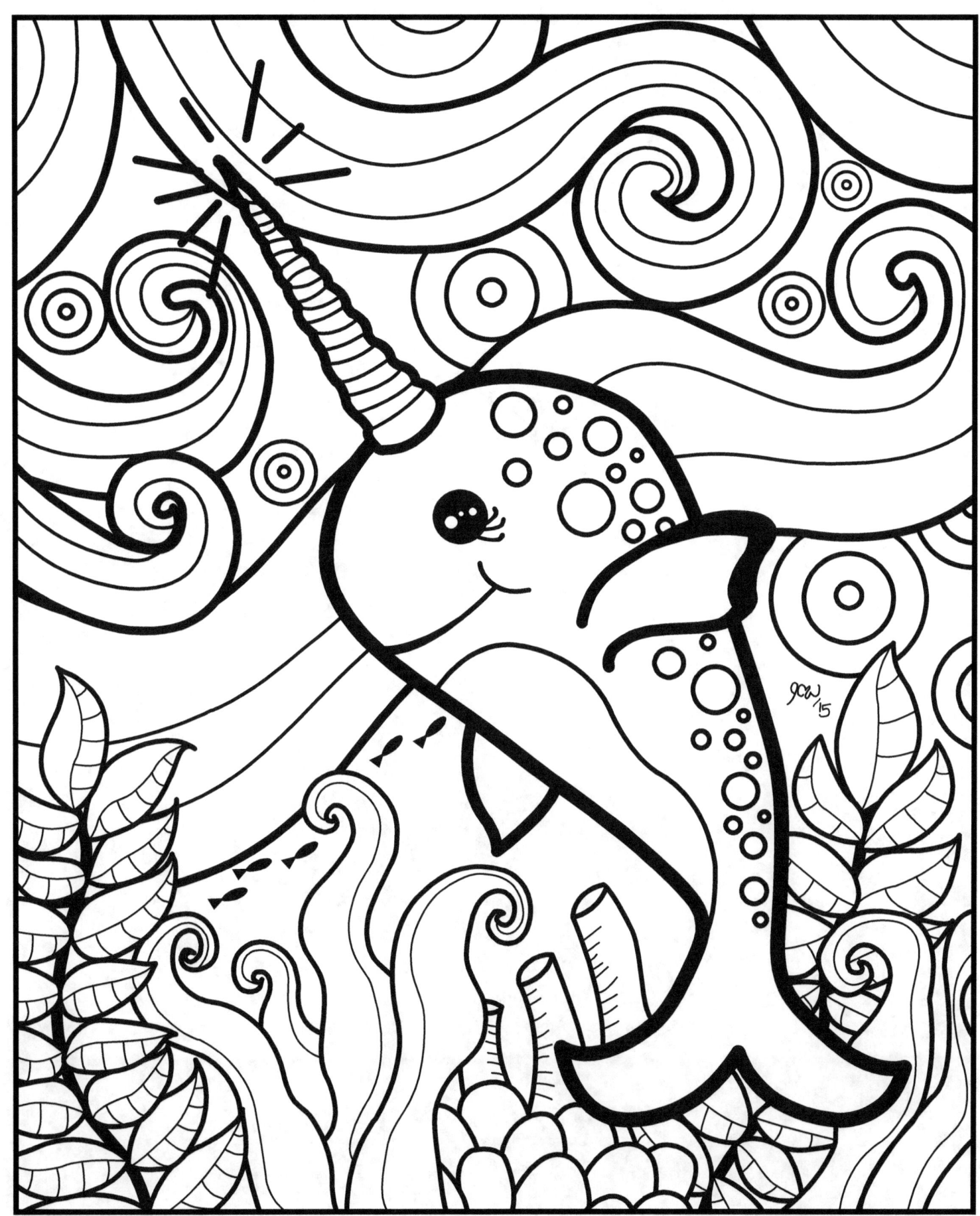

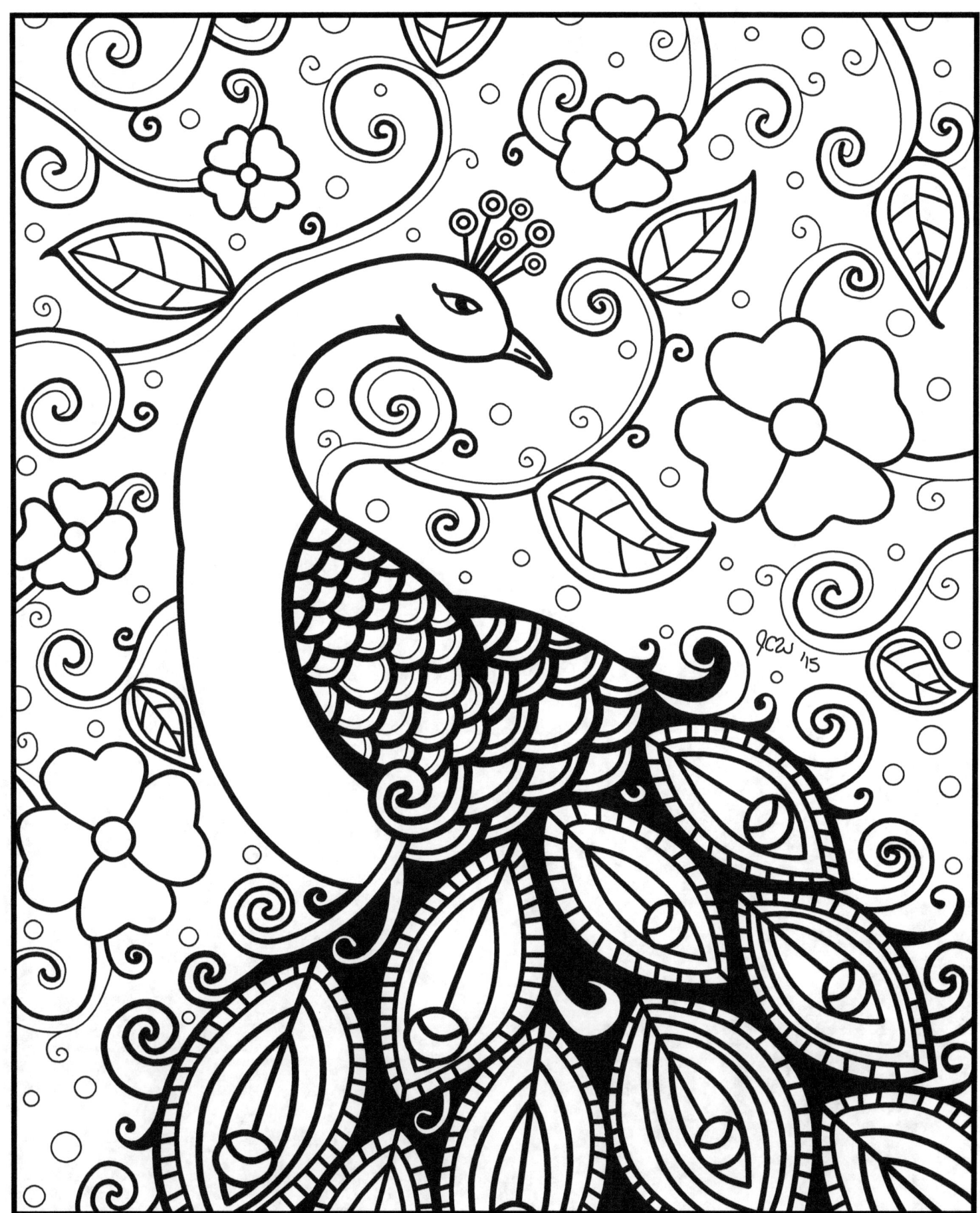

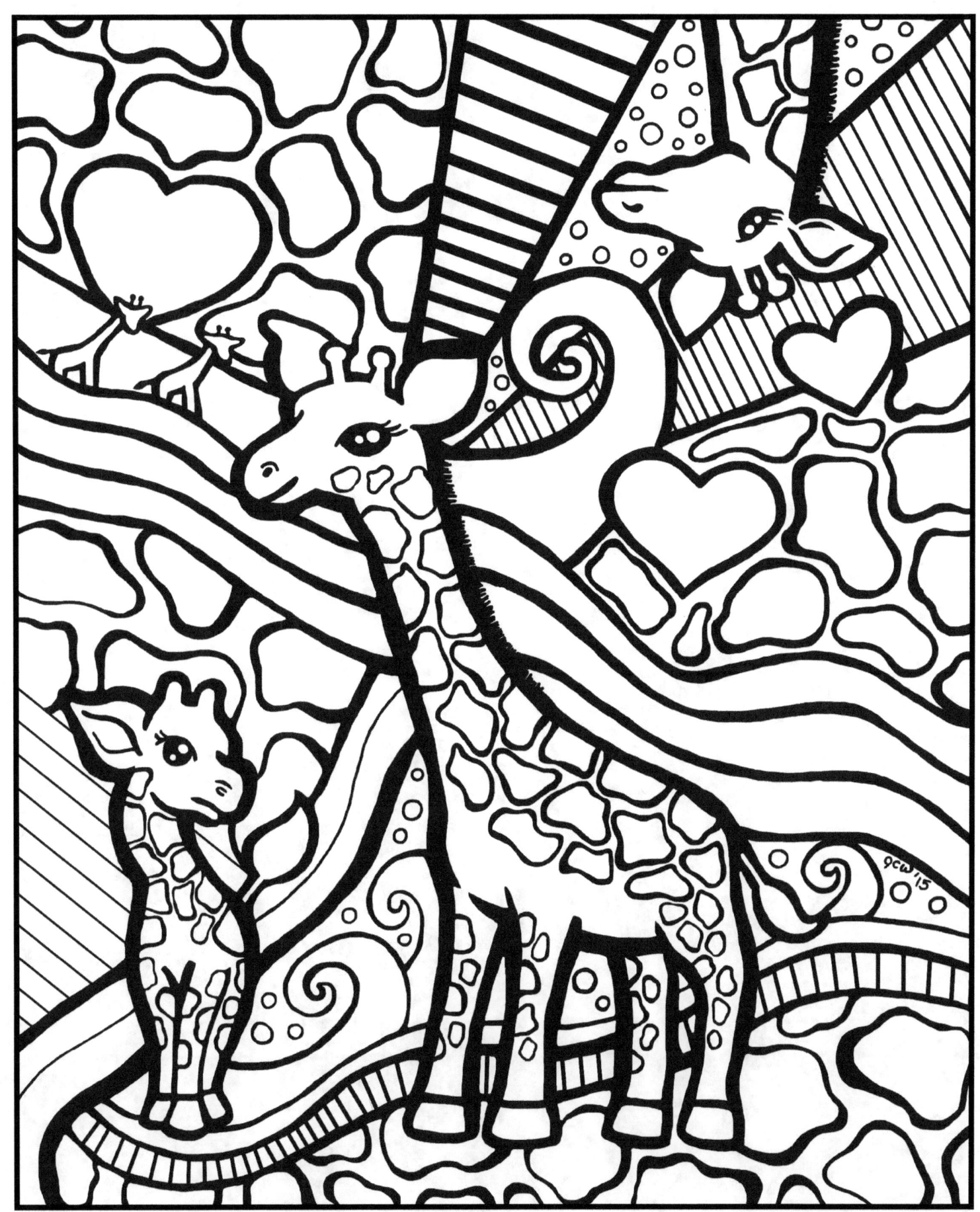

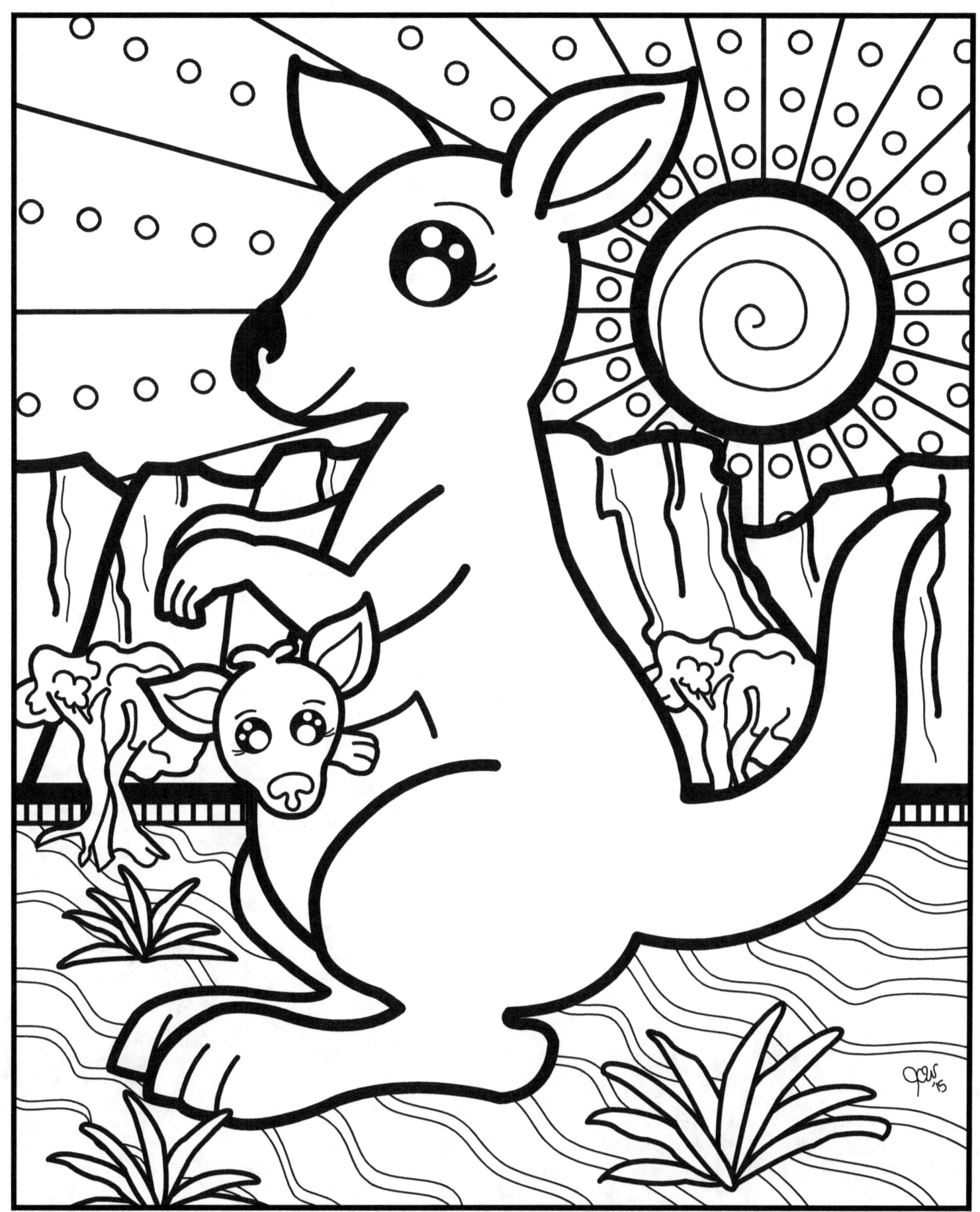

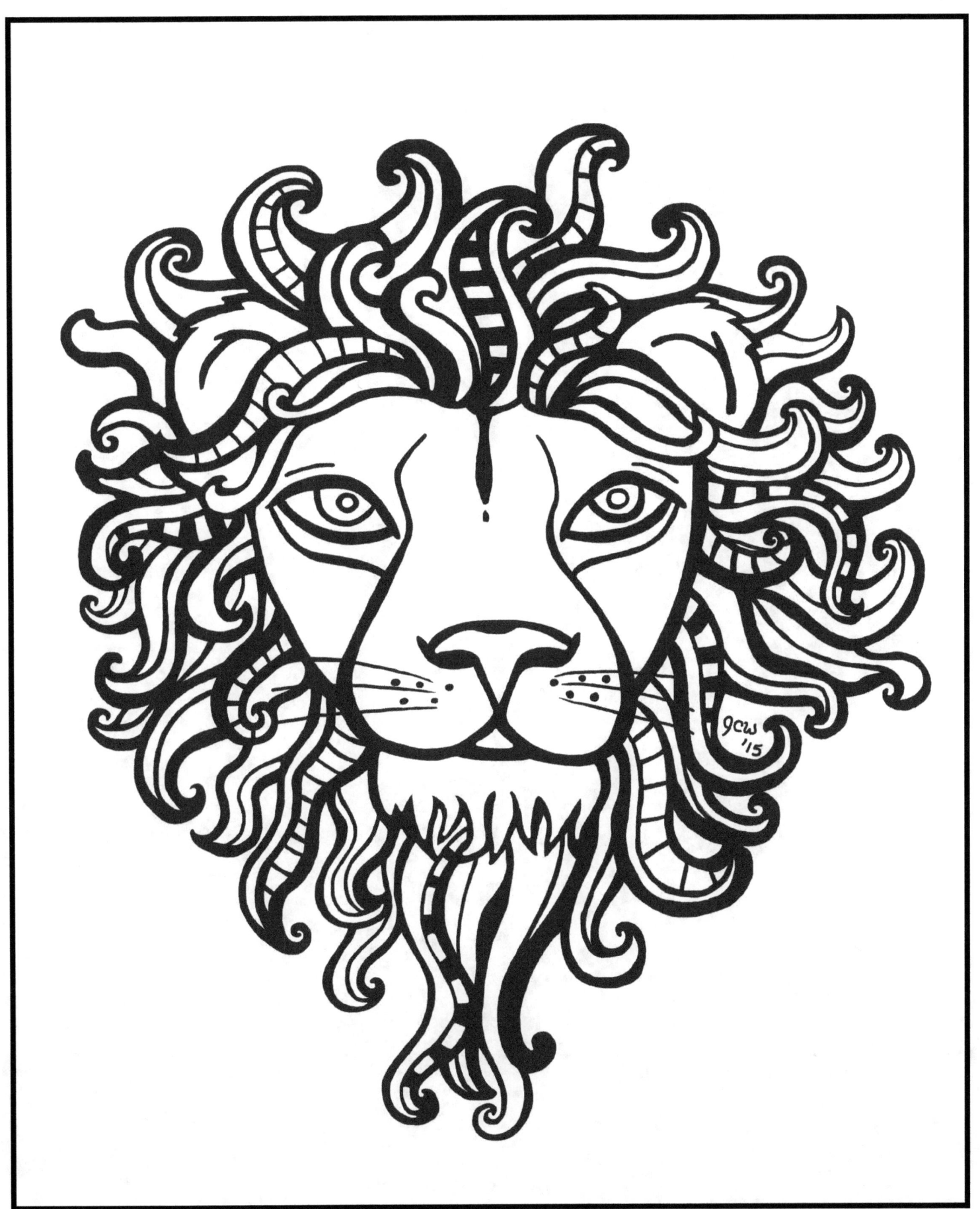

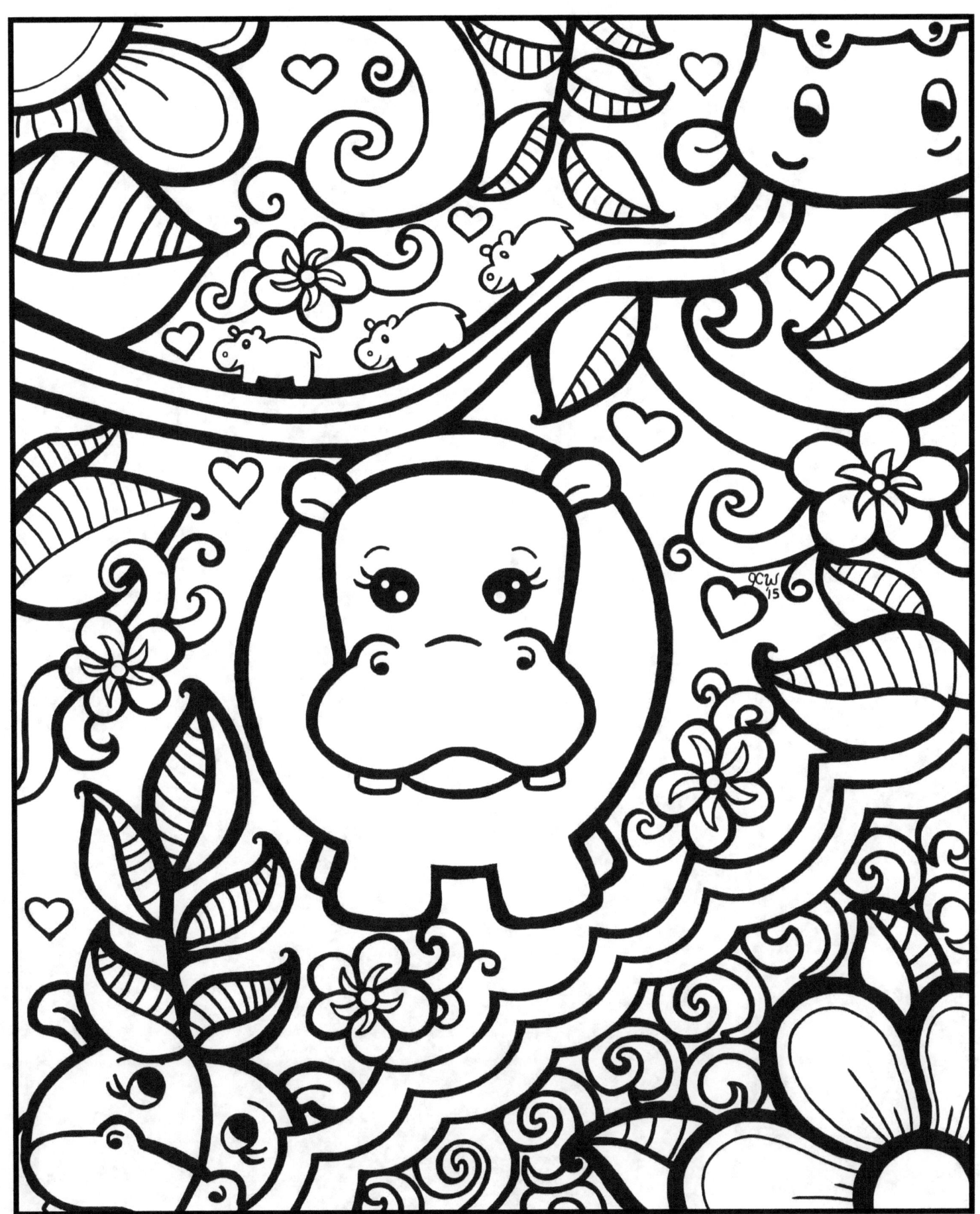

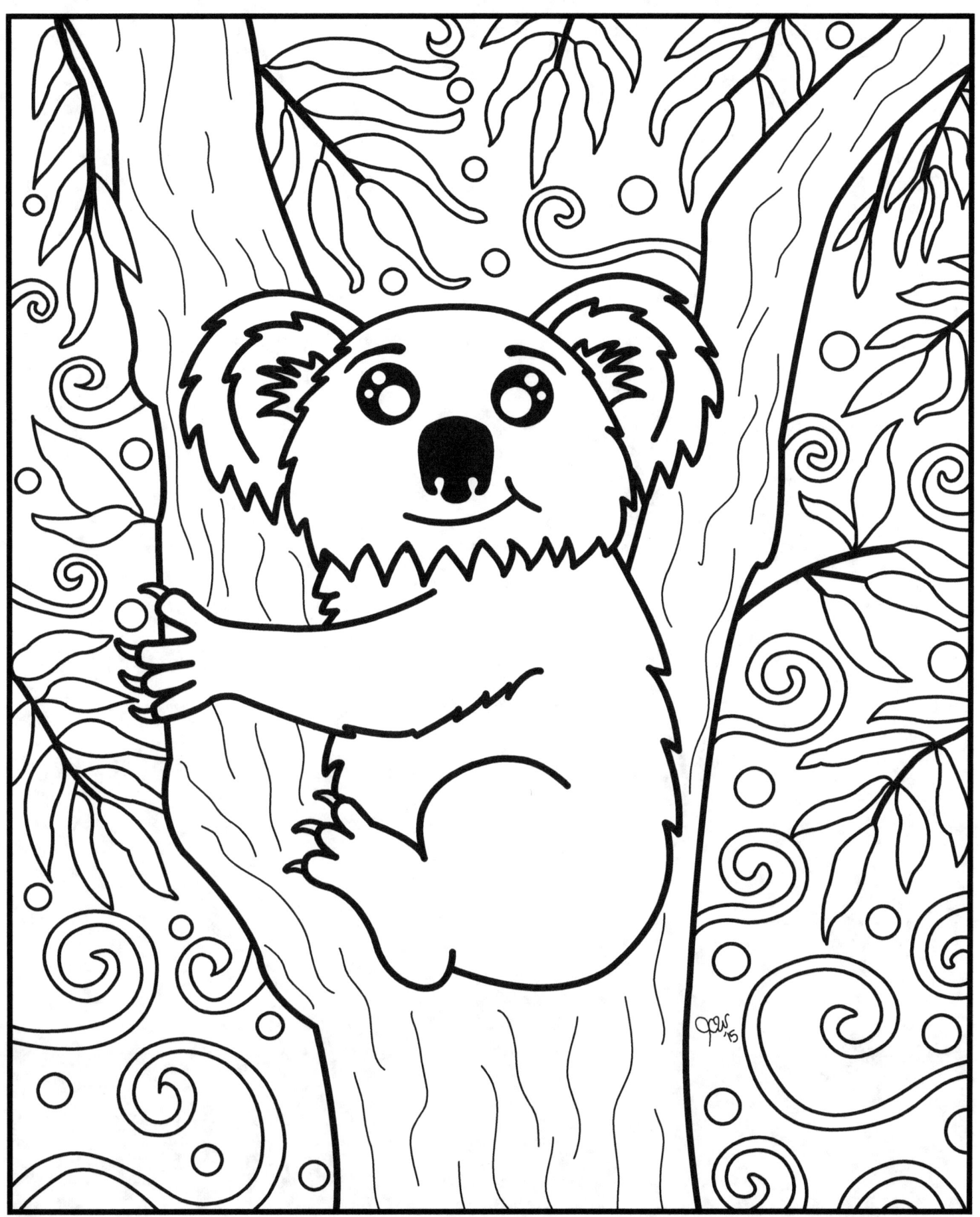

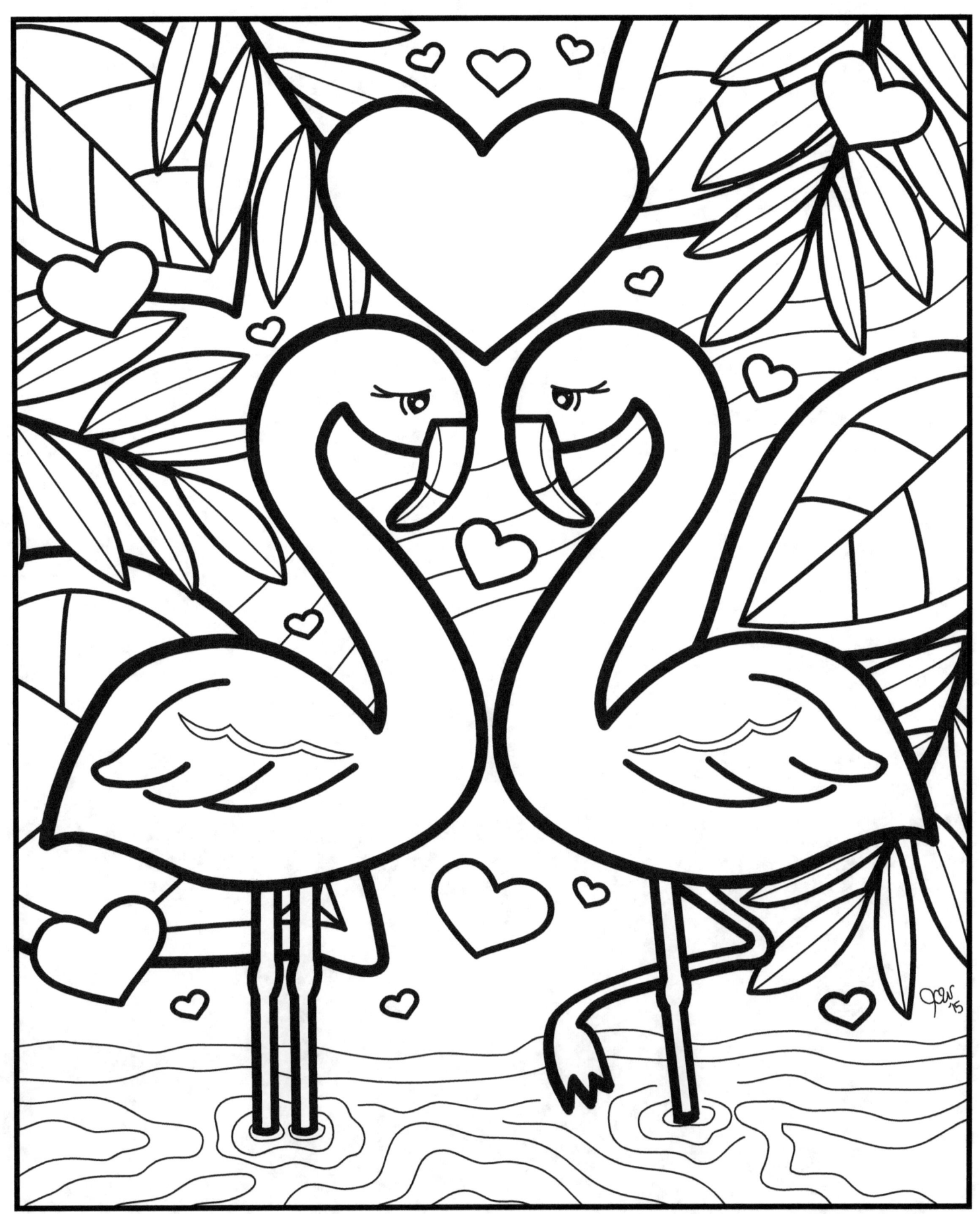

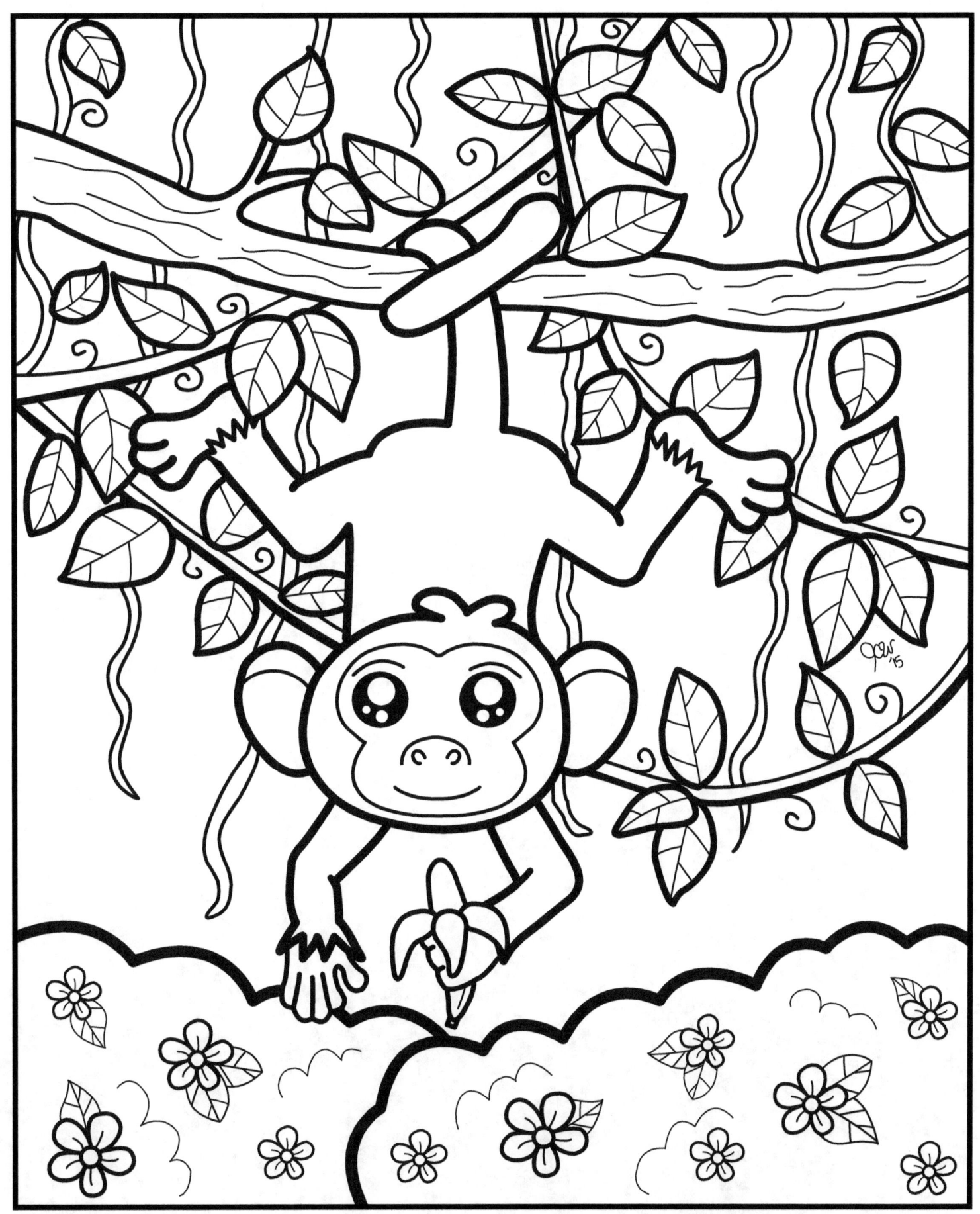

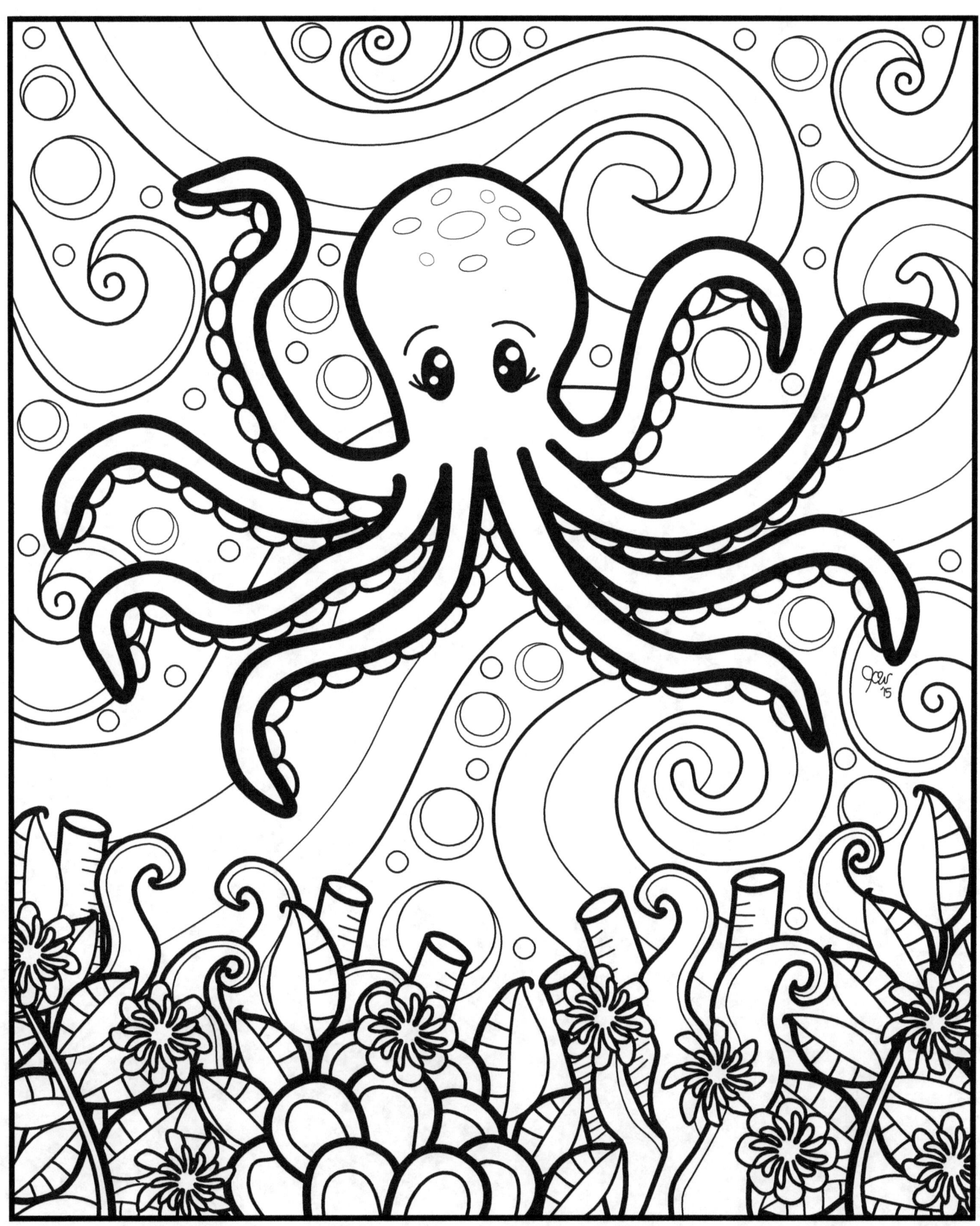

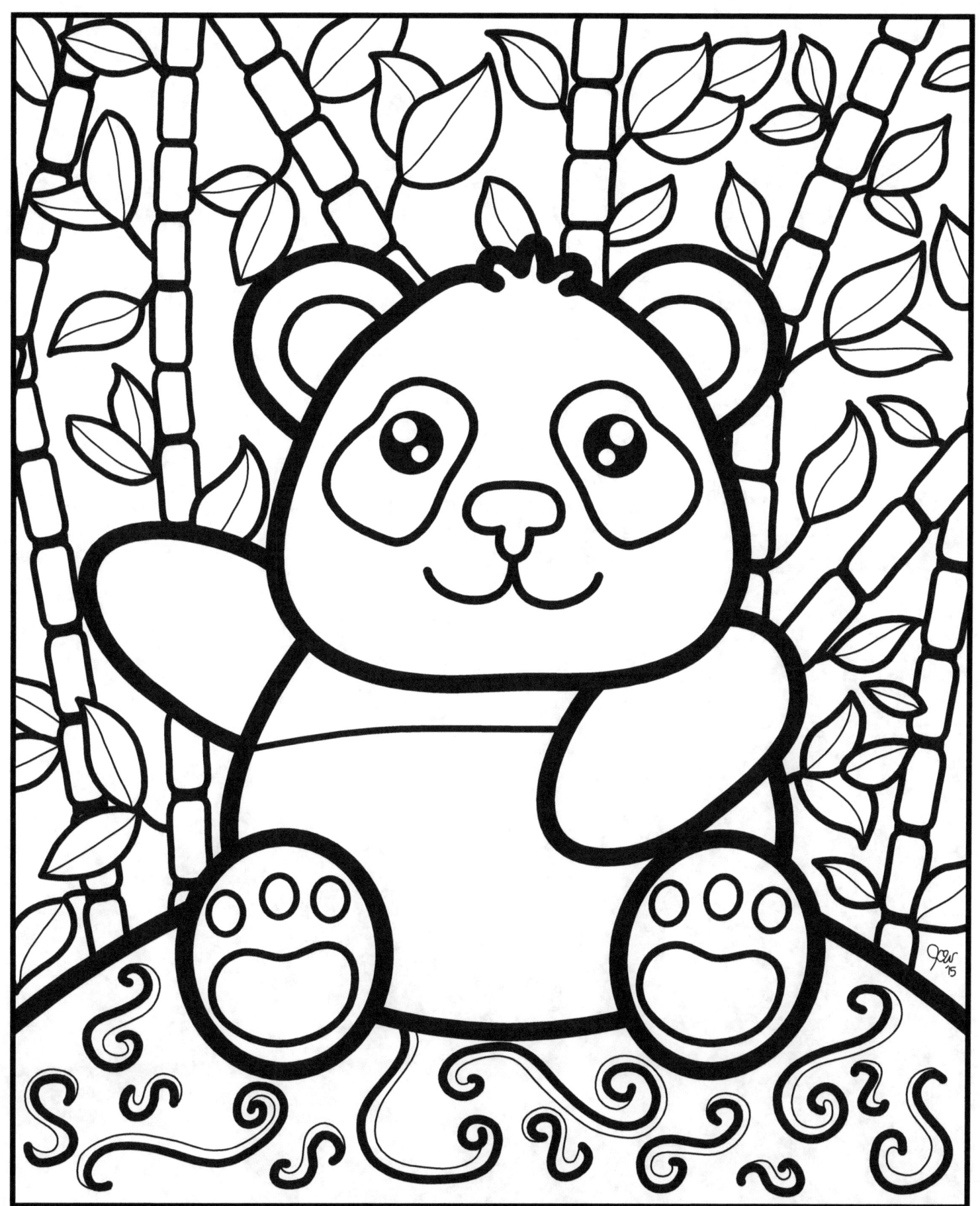

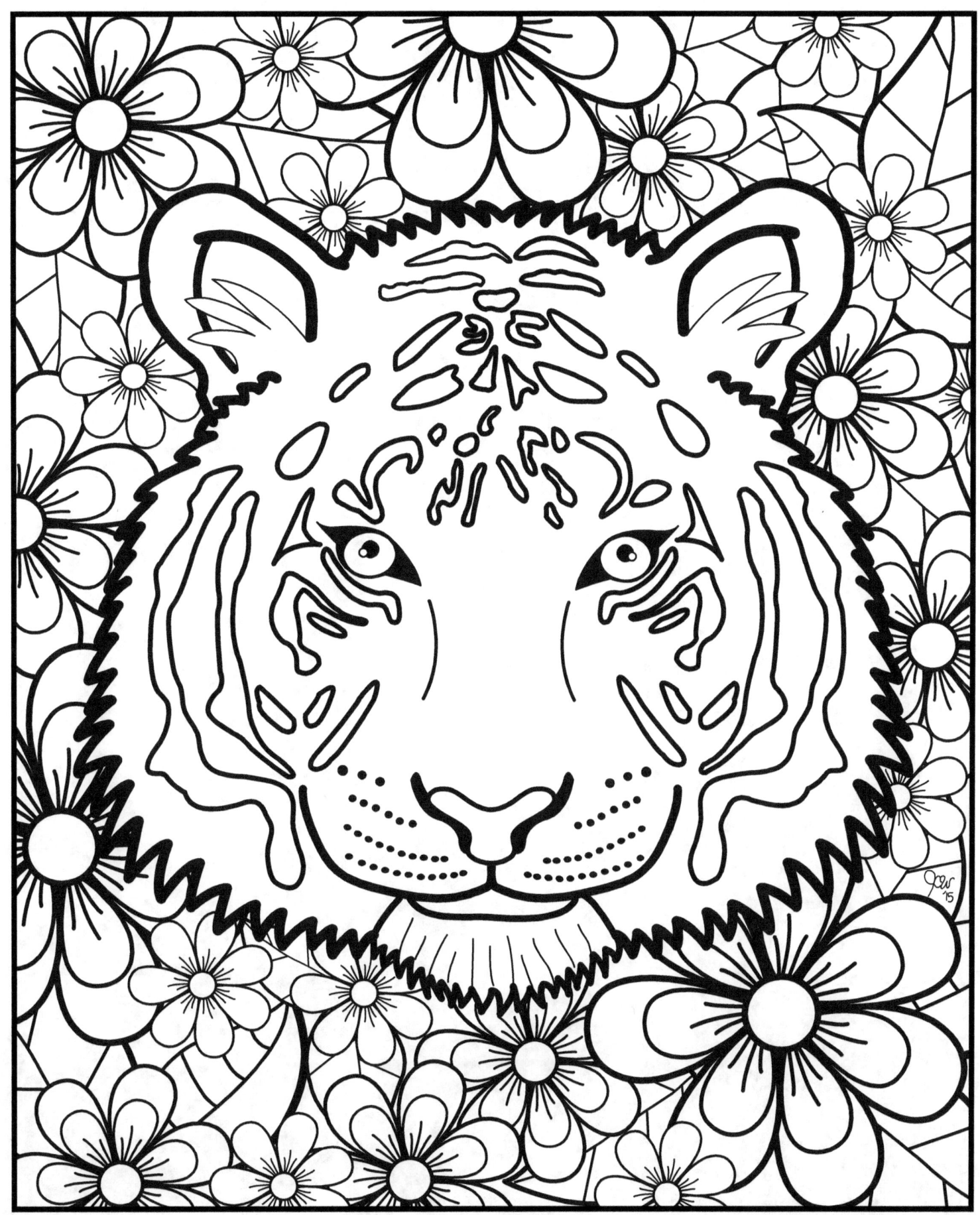

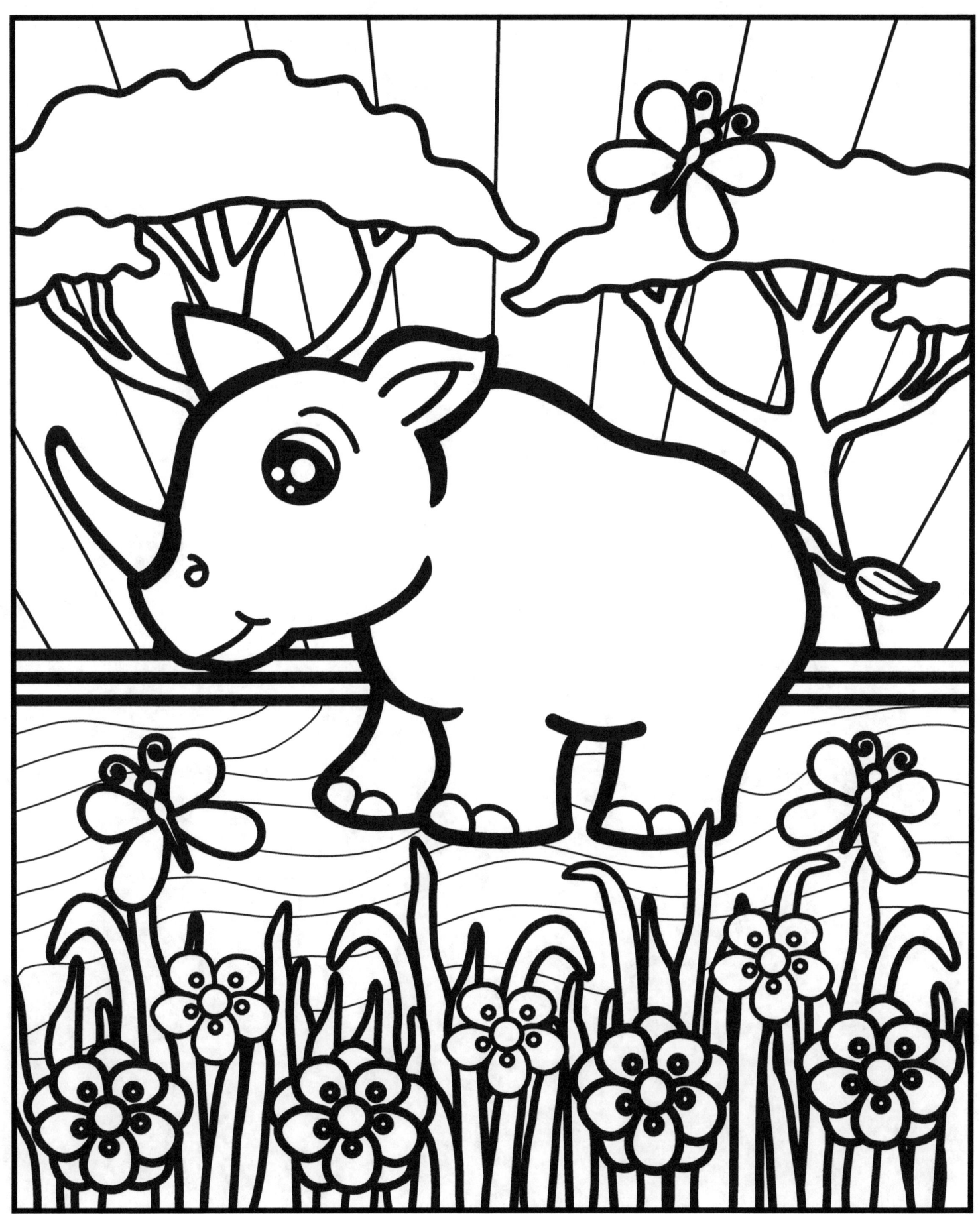

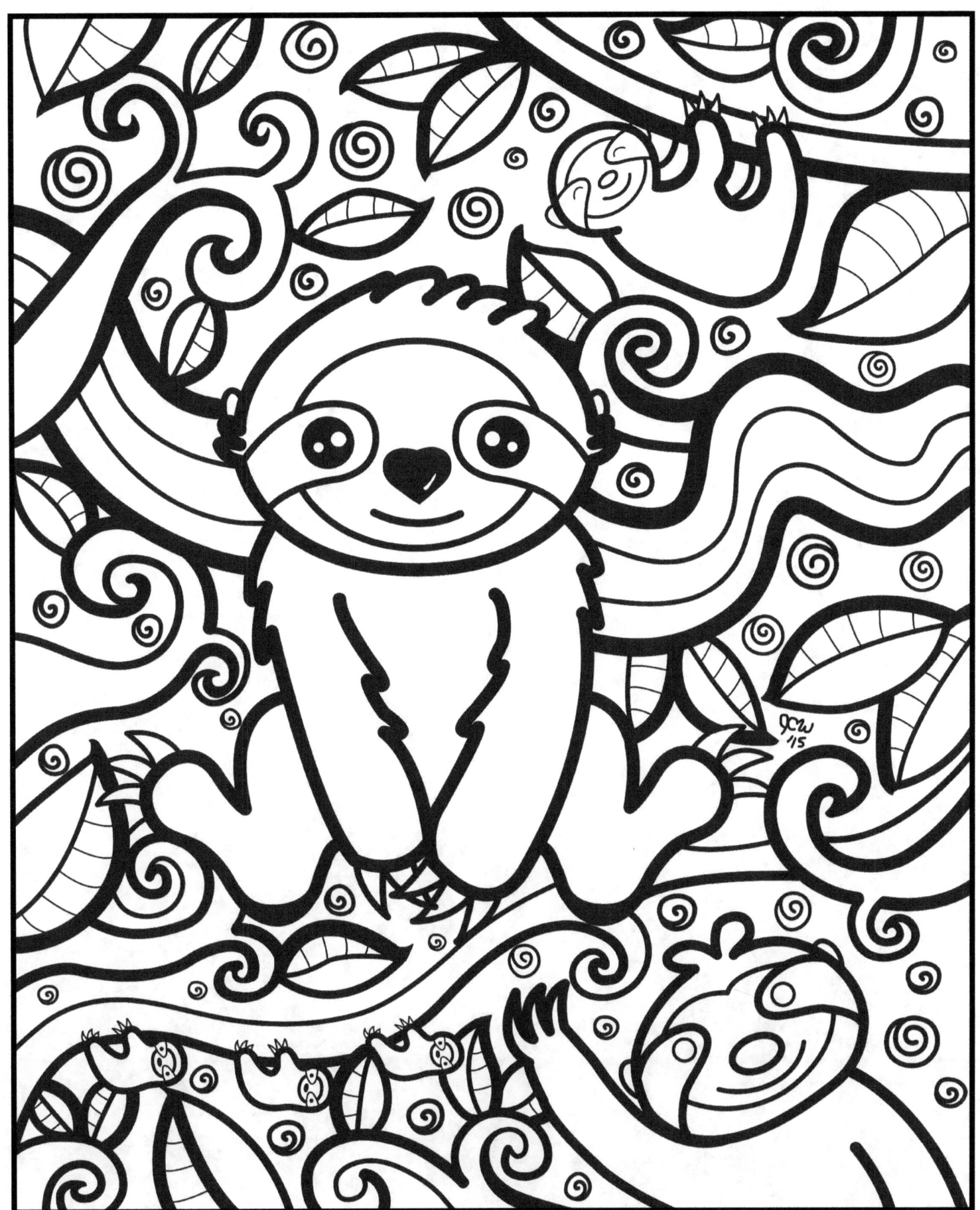

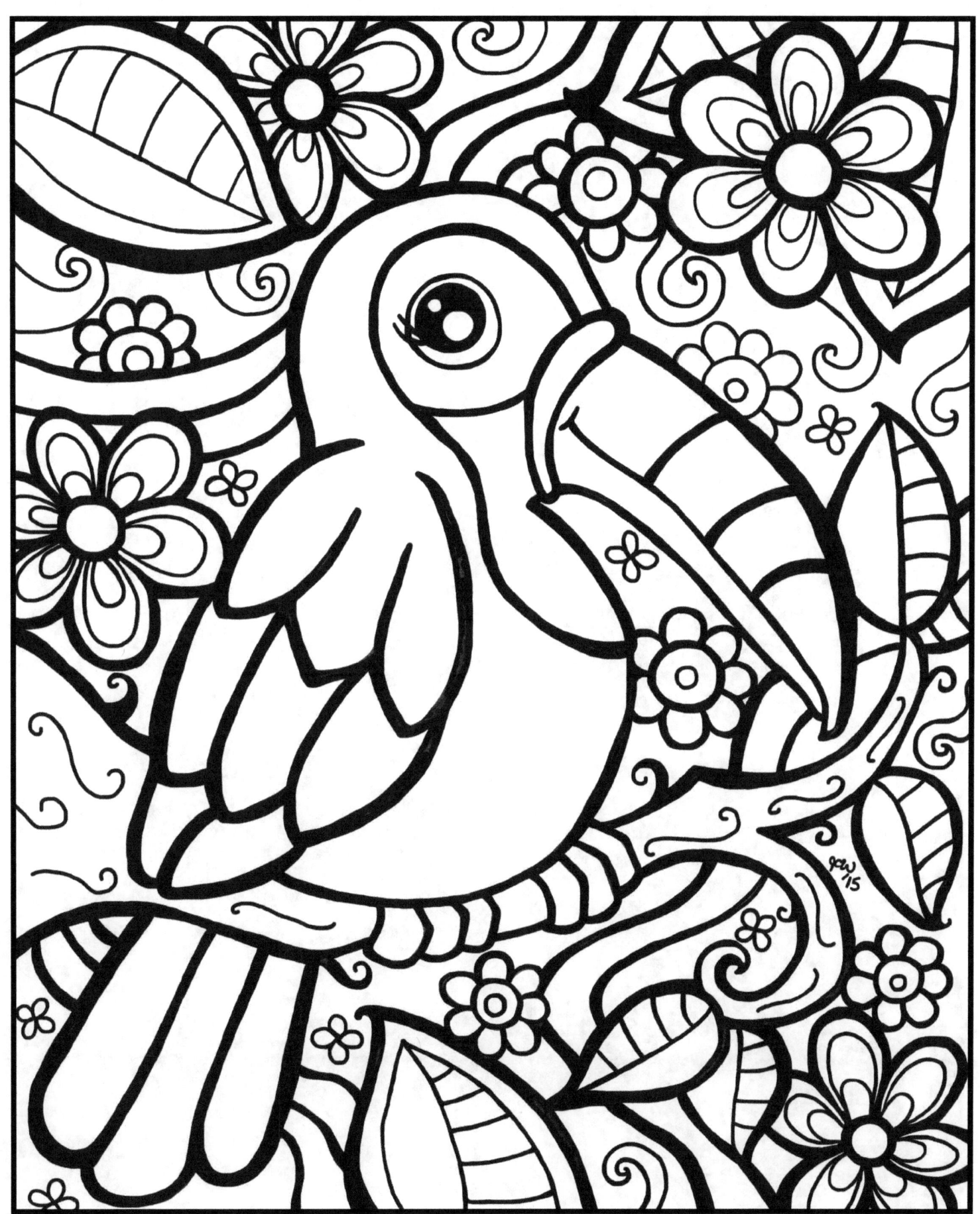

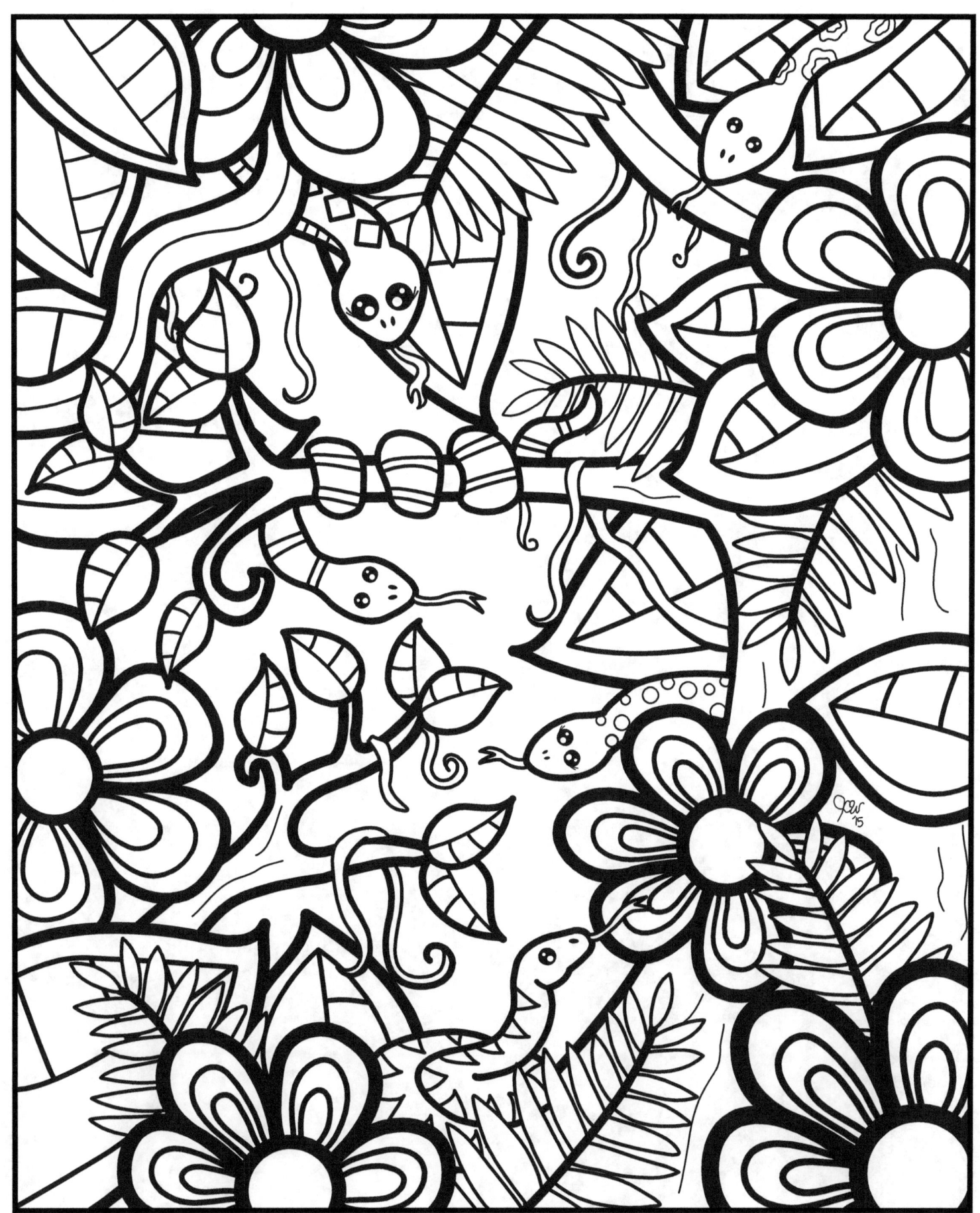

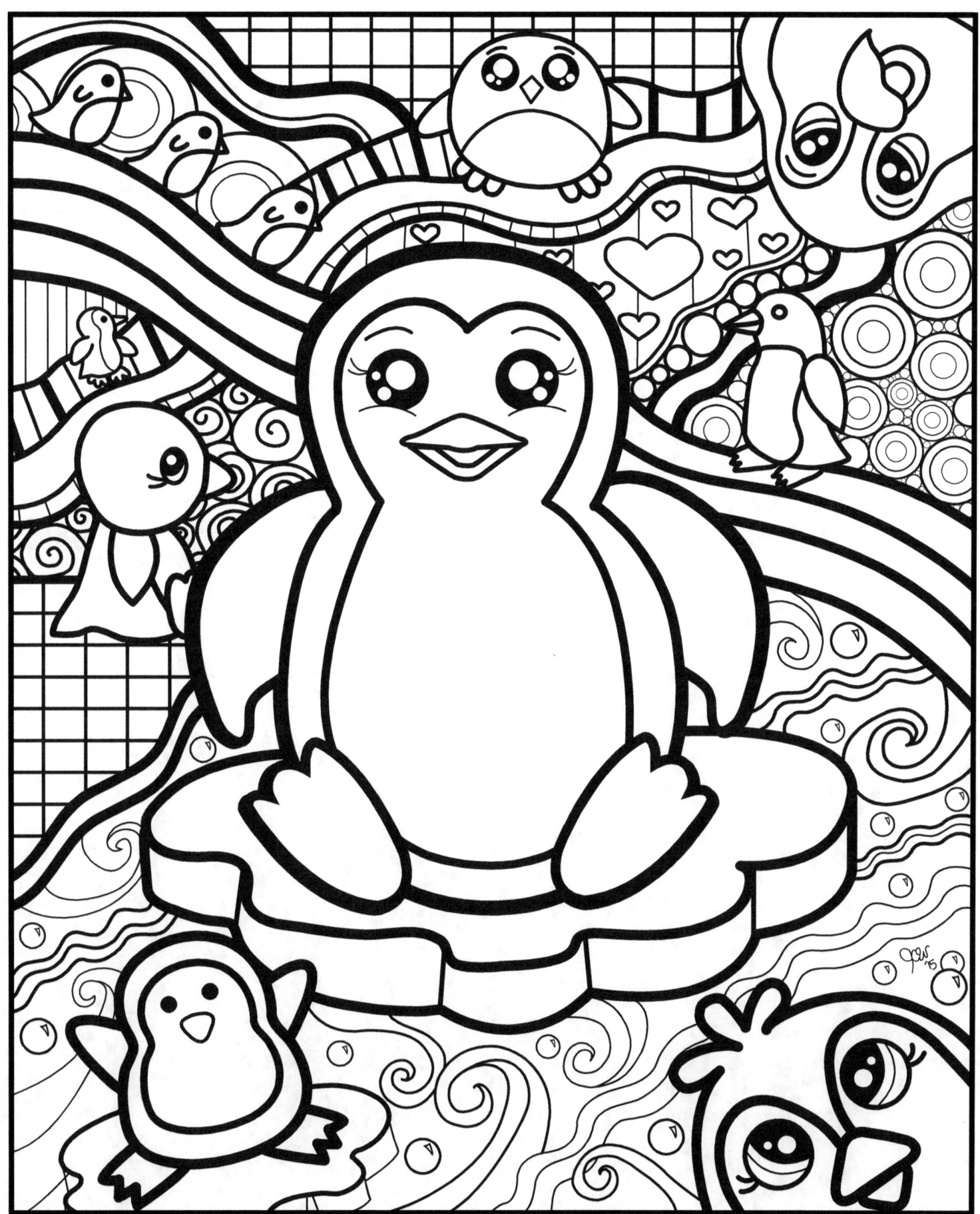

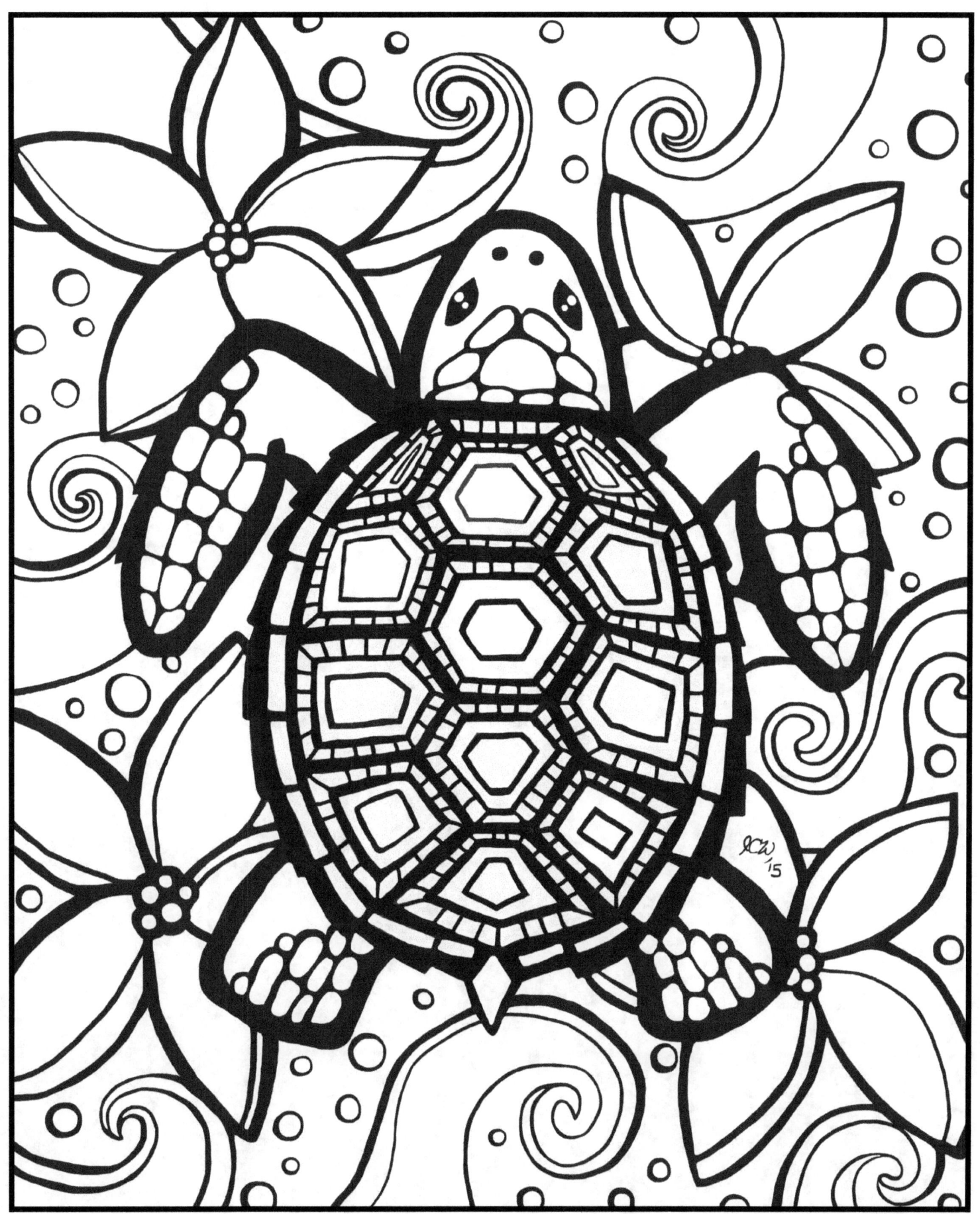

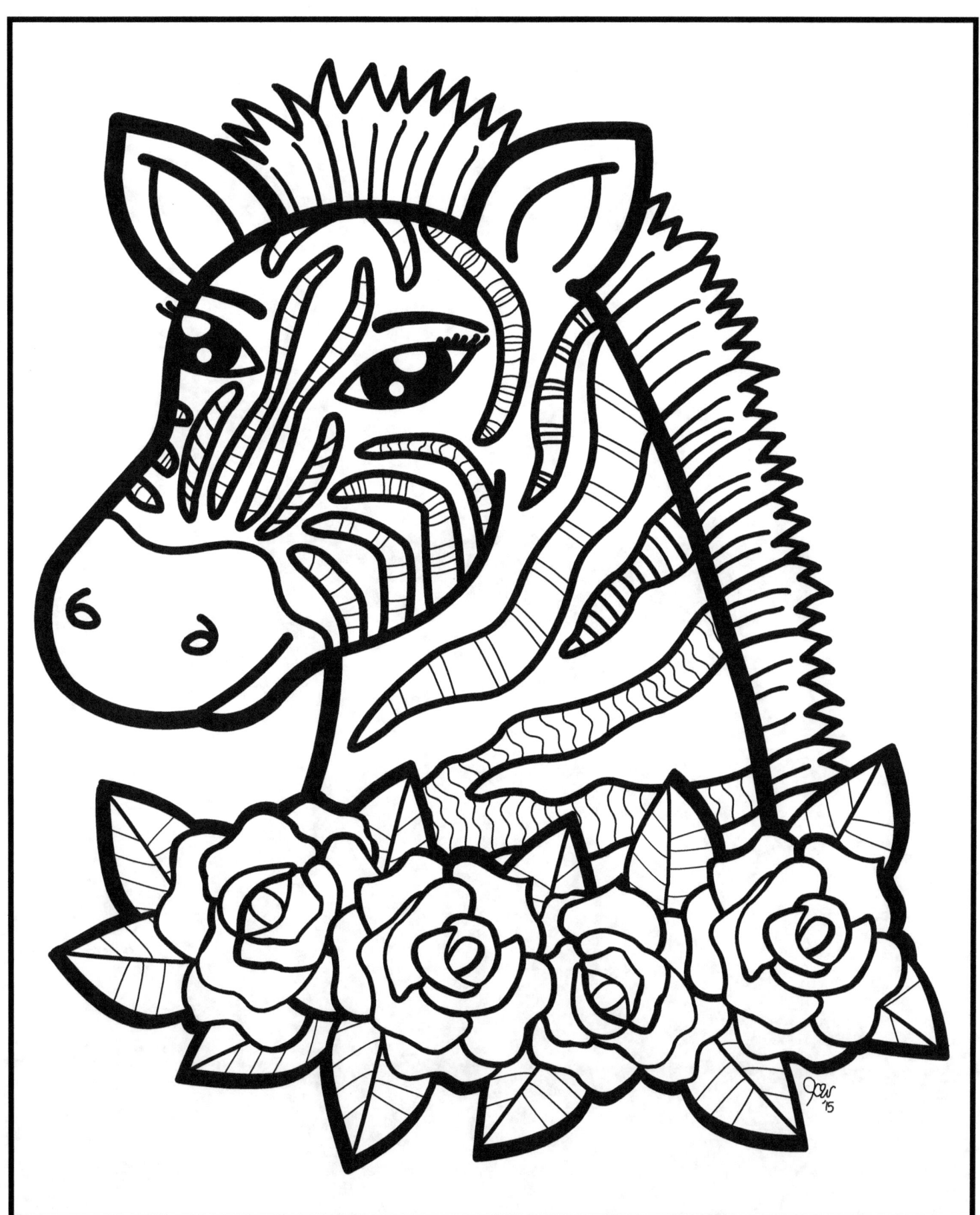